D1200323

DREAM JOBS IN
INFORMATION TECHNOLOGY

HELEN MASON

CRABTREE
PUBLISHING COMPANY
WWW.CRABTREEBOOKS.COM

CUTTING-EDGE CAREERS IN TECHNICAL EDUCATION

Author:
Helen Mason

Series research and development:
Reagan Miller

Editorial director:
Kathy Middleton

Editor:
Petrice Custance

Proofreader:
Lorna Notsch

Design, photo research, and prepress:
Katherine Berti

Print and production coordinator:
Katherine Berti

Photographs:
inspacewetrust.org
   Screen Shot 2018-03-12 at 3.26.43 p.m.:
   p. 23 (inset)
Shutterstock
   Bart Sadowski: p. 7 (center left)
   David M G: p. 22 (bottom)
   designs by Jack: p. 12 (Geek Squad logo)
   George W. Bailey: p. 21 (right)
   Keeton Gale: p. 28 (bottom)
   Ken Wolter: p. 12 (Skype logo)
   lev radin: p. 4 (center)
Stephen Reiach: p. 7 (bottom left)
All other images by Shutterstock

Library and Archives Canada Cataloguing in Publication

Mason, Helen, 1950-, author
       Dream jobs in information technology / Helen Mason.
(Cutting-edge careers in technical education)
Includes index.
Issued in print and electronic formats.
ISBN 978-0-7787-4438-2 (hardcover).--
ISBN 978-0-7787-4449-8 (softcover).--
ISBN 978-1-4271-2029-8 (HTML)
       1. Information technology--Vocational guidance--Juvenile literature.
2. Information technology--Employees--Training of--Juvenile literature.
I. Title.
HD9999.I492M38 2018   j004.023   C2018-900257-3
                                               C2018-900258-1

Library of Congress Cataloging-in-Publication Data

Available at the Library of Congress

Crabtree Publishing Company

www.crabtreebooks.com   1-800-387-7650

Printed in the U.S.A./052018/CG20180309

Published in Canada
Crabtree Publishing
616 Welland Ave.
St. Catharines, Ontario
L2M 5V6

Published in the United States
Crabtree Publishing
PMB 59051
350 Fifth Avenue, 59th Floor
New York, New York 10118

Published in the United Kingdom
Crabtree Publishing
Maritime House
Basin Road North, Hove
BN41 1WR

Published in Australia
Crabtree Publishing
3 Charles Street
Coburg North
VIC 3058

CONTENTS

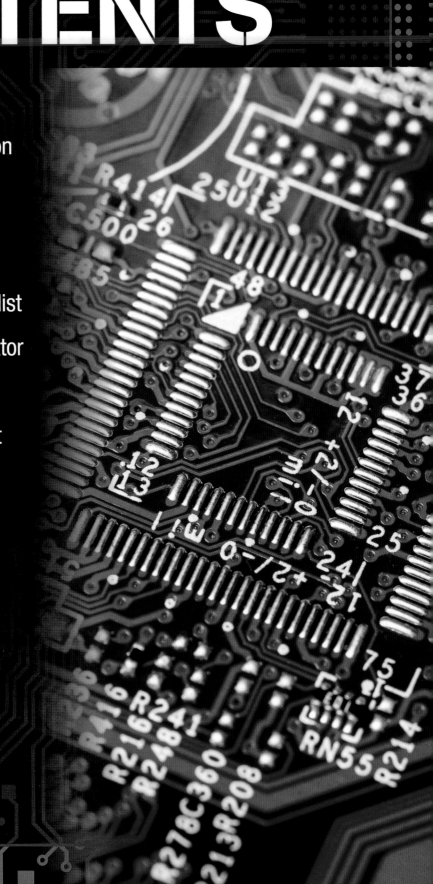

JOBS IN CAREER AND TECHNICAL EDUCATION

Career and Technical Education will equip you to do anything from drilling deep beneath Earth's surface for liquid gold to building computer systems for online stores around the world.

Do you like working with your hands? Do you enjoy figuring out how things work? Career and Technical Education (CTE) may be perfect for you.

WHAT IS CAREER AND TECHNICAL EDUCATION?

CTE programs combine academic studies, such as math and science, with valuable hands-on training. CTE students develop job-specific skills that are in high demand by employers.

CTE programs are divided into 16 career clusters. Some examples of these career clusters are Architecture and Construction, Law and Security, Health Sciences, Manufacturing, and Hospitality and Tourism. Each career cluster is divided into job pathways. Each job pathway is a grouping of jobs that require similar interests and paths of study. For example, in the Health Sciences CTE cluster, the Therapeutic Services pathway includes jobs such as registered nurse, home health aide, and dental assistant.

DID YOU KNOW?

Aarón Sánchez is a chef and television personality. His Aarón Sánchez Scholarship Fund helps Latin American students become chefs.

In 2016, the Hospitality and Tourism industry supported 7.6 million U.S. jobs.

In 2016, the construction industry provided more than 6.5 million jobs in the United States. By 2026, that number is expected to grow to more than 7.5 million.

WHY CTE?

Are you looking for a career that demands a combination of technical knowledge, critical thinking, initiative, and dedication? Do you enjoy solving problems and looking at things in new or different ways? Then you are an ideal candidate for CTE.

There are likely many different CTE programs being offered in your area. Search online or ask a trusted adult to help you find a program that matches your interests. Most high schools offer a wide range of CTE courses, and even some middle schools have them. You don't have to choose a career yet, but you can start to explore the exciting CTE options that are waiting for you.

Santa Fe Community College in Gainesville, Florida has a teaching zoo. Students can graduate with a degree in zoo animal technology.

CAREERS IN
INFORMATION TECHNOLOGY

A career in information technology involves working with computers and computer **applications**. You can build computer **networks** that reach around the world, design games that fill users with enthusiasm, and figure out ways to stop **hackers** from stealing sensitive data.

Information technology, or IT, refers to the development, maintenance, and use of computer systems, **software**, and networks for processing and distributing data. IT isn't confined to the laptop computer that sits on your desk, the iPad you carry, or your smartphone. IT runs the car or school bus that carries you to school. It is in the thermostat that maintains your school building at a comfortable temperature. IT runs the ovens that cook your meals and the machines that clean up afterward. When you are sick, computers help doctors diagnose what is wrong. Most people depend on IT in some way every single day—which means many job opportunities for you!

INFORMATION TECHNOLOGY JOB PATHWAYS:

NETWORK SYSTEMS	A network system is a computer operating system. Jobs in this area involve setting up and maintaining computer networks.
INFORMATION SUPPORT AND SERVICES	People in information support and services help you set up and use your computer and related software.
WEB AND DIGITAL COMMUNICATIONS	Web and digital communications workers create, design, and produce **multimedia** products and services.
PROGRAM AND SOFTWARE DEVELOPERS	Program and software developers design computer systems and software. This includes all of your favorite apps.

HOW TO USE THIS BOOK

Each two-page spread focuses on a specific career in the Information Technology CTE cluster. For each career, you will find a detailed description of life on the job, advice on the best educational path to take (see right), and tips on what you can do right now to begin preparing for your dream career. Let's get started!

YOUR PATH

SECONDARY SCHOOL

This section lists the best subjects to take in high school.

POST-SECONDARY

Some jobs require an **apprenticeship** and **certification** while others require a college or university degree. This section gives you an idea of the best path to take after high school.

The **database** at this **stock exchange** integrates data from exchanges all over the world.

Music software developers create the programs that help your favorite band rock.

Network administrators are responsible for all wireless and **remote access** devices in your school.

This **postproduction** film editor reviews multiple versions of each scene before choosing one.

NETWORK
ARCHITECT

Computer network architects design and build data communications networks.

The demand for network architects continues to grow as businesses and firms increase their use of information technology. Today, such networks help businesses communicate both with staff and with clients. They also run machinery, keep track of inventory, and handle accounts.

ON THE JOB

The exciting thing about being a network architect is that you get to work with so many different people and so much technology. In this job, you'll interview customers, plus sales and marketing staff, to help you understand your company's current computer needs and how these needs may change. You plan computer networks that meet both current and future needs. You present these plans to managers and explain the pluses and minuses of your ideas. Once a plan has been okayed, you work with **hardware** engineers and installers to build and put in the system. As the business grows and computer demands increase, you adjust the size of the network. You also research new technologies and upgrade **routers**, **adaptors**, software, and security systems. In addition, you troubleshoot and repair network problems.

Computer network architects work on **LANs**, **WANs**, **intranets**, and **extranets** (see below).

DID YOU KNOW?

There are four types of networks. LANs, or local area networks, connect people in a single building or connected group of buildings. WANs connect people in a wide public network, such as the telephone system. Intranets are restricted networks used for sharing company information. Extranets are private networks open to authorized users, such as suppliers, vendors, and customers.

WHAT CAN YOU DO NOW?

Develop skills now by joining a computer club or volunteering to assist in your school's computer lab. Learn all you can about **computer coding**. Research the different kinds of computer networks, software, and hardware.

This network architect plans how to maintain, repair, and upgrade a network without disrupting service.

YOUR PATH TO WORK AS A NETWORK ARCHITECT

SECONDARY SCHOOL

Math, computer, science, social studies, and business courses are a great start.

POST-SECONDARY

A university degree in computer science, information systems, or engineering is required.

DID YOU KNOW?

The Information Technology Association of Canada (ITAC) wants more female, **Indigenous**, immigrant, and differently abled students to pursue IT careers. Its Career Ready Program provides students with work placements and valuable training.

■	$110,680–$125,340
■	$99,920–$109,750
■	$89,200–$98,780
■	$50,530–$89,040

This 2016 map shows the average annual salary for network architects across the United States.

IT MANAGER

IT managers oversee all of the computer-related activities in an organization.

In 2017, more than half of Americans preferred shopping online. The rising number of online shoppers means the number of IT management positions will grow. Businesses need these experts to provide custom-designed online experiences to their customers. They want managers who can plan **interactive** websites that load quickly and checkouts that work on both desktop computers and mobile devices.

ON THE JOB

IT managers figure out what computer equipment and systems their organization needs. When necessary, they plan to expand the system. They assess the costs and benefits of upgrades and present them to management. IT managers also assess what technical support upgrades will need and how to provide this support to internal staff and customers. They arrange to install the necessary hardware and software and negotiate with vendors to get the best prices.

This IT manager provides support for one of Thailand's business hotel and restaurant operations.

This sales manager forgot an important file in his home office. Thanks to remote accessing, he can download it at the airport.

YOUR PATH TO WORK AS AN IT MANAGER

SECONDARY SCHOOL

Focus on math, computers, science, social studies, and business courses.

POST-SECONDARY

A university degree in a computer or information science field is necessary.

THE WORKPLACE

The specifics of an IT management job vary depending on the type of business involved. At a bank, you might figure out how to convince teens to open an account at your bank one day and research how to sell investments to retirees another. Alternatively, you may work for a computer systems design company, an insurance corporation, information company, manufacturer, or a government agency.

WHAT CAN YOU DO NOW?

Get a head start by volunteering to assist in your school's computer lab. Join a speech or debate club to develop your communication skills.

DID YOU KNOW?

In 2015, 3.7 million Americans worked from a home office at least half of the week. IT managers use remote accessing software tools such as GoToMyPC or TeamViewer to sort out technical troubles.

The IT manager for this firm maintains all voice, video, and data connections with drivers who travel right across the country. "You will make mistakes," the IT manager says. "The key is to learn from them."

USER SUPPORT
SPECIALIST

User support specialists help people who are having difficulties with their computer software and equipment.

As a user support specialist, you work directly with people and organizations. Many people don't bother reading software instruction manuals and find online help frustrating. Your job is to talk them through the steps of getting their equipment or software working. Sometimes this will be in person. At other times, you'll be talking on the telephone or even online.

Consumers want support staff who can solve their problem quickly in a friendly and knowledgeable way.

ON THE JOB

No matter how much or how little users know about computer equipment and software, they can run into problems. As a user support specialist, it's your job to listen to customers' descriptions of their difficulties. You ask questions to help diagnose the problem and then walk them through problem-solving steps to help solve it. You read technical manuals to make sure you understand all you can about equipment and software. This helps when you train users to work with new hardware and software. Don't be surprised if your bosses ask what gives customers the most trouble. Your feedback will assist in developing new training materials and procedures.

DID YOU KNOW?

Many user support specialists have spent hours on the telephone trying to talk a customer through a problem ... only to discover during an on-site visit that the power cable isn't plugged into the back of the equipment!

THE WORKPLACE

You will likely work in a call center that focuses on online or telephone support. This center may be run by a software company or by a business that handles support for several brands. Alternatively, you may troubleshoot computer problems for a school or college.

WHAT CAN YOU DO NOW?

Develop your computer coaching skills by joining your school's audiovisual club. Volunteer at an after-school drop-in or seniors' center, where you can assist people with software issues.

SECONDARY SCHOOL

Focus on math, computers, science, social studies, English, and business courses.

POST-SECONDARY

Requirements vary from online courses to a university degree in a computer-related field.

People in user support must have excellent verbal and written communication skills. Joining a speech or drama club is an excellent way to develop these necessary skills.

By 2018, 86 percent of businesses are expected to use **teleconferencing**. Support staff make sure employees can access and participate in online meetings.

DATABASE
ADMINISTRATOR

Database administrators, or DBAs, have three basic tasks: protect the data, protect the data, and protect the data.

In August 2017, a supplier of voting machines failed to use a password to protect the names, addresses, birthdates, and partial social security numbers of 1.8 million Illinois residents. That same month, a Minnesota school board accidently included the grades and identification numbers of 9,000 students in an e-mail about bus routes. As a database administrator, your job is to prevent such things from happening! This involves using **firewalls** and **encryption** to prevent the wrong people from accessing data. At the same time, you must allow authorized users to access it.

ON THE JOB

You ensure that databases are efficient and error-free. You back up all data and keep the backup in a secure location so that you can restore data in case of a power outage or natural disaster. As you learn about better ways to organize, you modify your system. You test all changes to make sure that things continue to run smoothly. You also do regular checks to make sure that only people with the correct permissions have access to database information.

This fake pop-up message attempts to scare people into clicking on links so hackers can gain access to their system. DBAs must be aware of such scams and how to avoid them.

WHAT CAN YOU DO NOW?

Assist one of your school's sports teams in keeping track of the data from their games and players. Research methods for how to protect data. Join a computer club or start your own. Learn all you can about database systems, firewalls, and methods of encryption. Search online for tutorials or activities dealing with computer systems security.

DBAs try to hack their own system. If they can do it, so can others.

Malware
cker
Identity Theft
Remote Admin
Phishing
Backdoor
Password
Crime
Virus Computer
Spam
Botnet
Social Netw
E-Commerce
Fraud
Update
Worms
Internet Scam
Username
Skimming

YOUR PATH TO WORK AS A DATABASE ADMINISTRATOR

SECONDARY SCHOOL

Math, computer, science, and social studies classes are a great start.

POST-SECONDARY

A university degree in computer science, information technology, or management information systems is required.

DID YOU KNOW?

In 1995, Kevin Mitnick went to jail for hacking dozens of computer networks. After serving his time, he now advises corporations and governments on systems security issues.

DID YOU KNOW?

Google paid high school student Ezequiel Pereira $10,000 for finding and reporting a security problem in its App Engine.

Security breaches can occur at any time. Top DBAs are on call at all times.

TECHNICAL WRITER

Technical writers create how-to information in simple language that anyone can understand.

You can explain how to run a computer system so clearly that anyone can understand it. This includes those who are just getting into computing and students who've been using it since they were two or three. There's a rising need for people with such skills as consumers demand more web-based products and developers create more products for the scientific and technical markets.

ON THE JOB

You explain complex and technical information in understandable language. You figure out what users need in order to run technical systems. To do that, you study the systems themselves and talk to both designers and developers. You may help them make a product easier to use so it needs fewer instructions. You consider whether to use paper-based or digital support. Often you develop both, using photographs, drawings, diagrams, animation, and charts to increase user understanding. As well as instruction manuals and how-to guides, you author computer journal articles, **FAQ**s, and animations. You edit each draft until the text is simple and clear. As you get feedback from users, you make revisions.

Technical writers don't have to be computer experts. They need to know what questions to ask and where to get the answers.

Technical writers check all instructions. Are they clear? Do they include all of the necessary information?

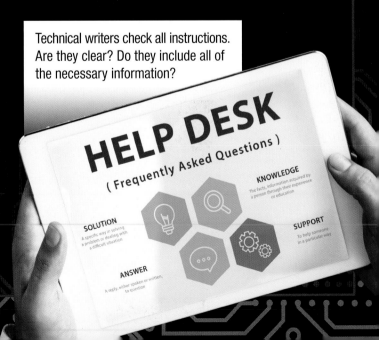

WHAT CAN YOU DO NOW?

Volunteer to coach people of different ages in computer software or online use. Notice what kind of coaching seems to work best for them. Join a speech or drama club to improve your communication skills. Start writing articles for your school newspaper or an online kids' blog to sharpen your writing skills. Start reading instruction manuals and notice the kind of language and style those technical writers used.

YOUR PATH TO WORK AS A TECHNICAL WRITER

SECONDARY SCHOOL

Literature, math, computer, science, and social studies are highly recommended.

POST-SECONDARY

A college or university degree in fields related to engineering, computer science, medicine, or web design is often required.

Writers listen to reports from user support specialists. Repeated questions from customers may signal a problem in the manual.

Many consumers prefer video instructions. Technical writers learn to use software such as Captivate to create video tutorials.

DID YOU KNOW?

In 2016, many technical writers earned between $50,000 and $70,000 a year, while some experienced technical writers earned up to $150,000.

Video Tutorial

1:03/2:56

CYBERSECURITY
EXPERT

Security experts protect computers against hackers and other attacks.

In 2016, an average of 4,000 **ransomware** attacks occurred each day. Attacks doubled during the first part of 2017 and continue to climb. No wonder openings in this field are projected to grow 37 percent by 2022.

ON THE JOB

As a security expert, you plan and implement methods that protect computer networks and systems. You protect computer files against accidental or unauthorized modifications, destruction, or access. You research new computer viruses and update your firm's virus detection systems to block them. You install and use firewalls and data encryption programs. You monitor computer networks for security breaches. When these occur, you investigate them, document the extent of any damage, and block future attacks. You work to keep ahead of **cyber attackers** by simulating attacks on your own systems and assessing what weaknesses someone might exploit. You keep abreast of the latest IT security trends and develop recovery plans in case your system suffers a major attack.

Security experts coach computer users in how to install and use new security programs.

In June 2017, a **keylogger virus** installed on a computer at the San Antonio Institute of Women's Health picked up every keystroke. Hackers got access to the personal and financial information of patients.

DID YOU KNOW?

The first computer worm was developed by a student to help him determine the size of cyberspace. When the worm encountered a **critical error**, it changed into a virus that damaged 6,000 computers and cost millions in repair bills.

WHAT CAN YOU DO NOW?

Study computer coding. Learn all you can about the different forms of cyber attacks and cybersecurity. Join a computer club. Enter a computer programming competition to develop your computer skills. SkillsUSA and Skills Canada offer many different competitions for students throughout the year.

DID YOU KNOW?

October is National Cyber Security Awareness month. STOP. THINK. CONNECT. is a campaign that helps kids be safe online. Some of its securty tips include how to set strong passwords and privacy settings, how to protect personal data, warnings to never click on links you are not sure of, and what to do if someone makes you feel uncomfortable online.

YOUR PATH TO WORK AS A CYBERSECURITY EXPERT

SECONDARY SCHOOL

Focus on math, computers, science, and social studies.

POST-SECONDARY

A university degree in computer science, programming, or a related field is required.

In 2015, Americans paid $24 million in ransomware payments. By 2016, payments were in the billion dollar range.

Ooops, your files have been encrypted!

To regain access to your files, you must pay $500 in two days or your files will be destroyed.

Payment must be received in
47:32:54
Time Left

Files will be lost in
47:34:54
Time Left

About Bitcoin

How to buy Bitcoin?

Contact Us

bitcoin ACCEPT HERE

Copy

Check Payment   **Decrypt**

ANIMATOR

Animators create characters that appear to come to life on-screen.

Computer animators work in a variety of exciting industries. These include gaming, entertainment, interior design, architecture, medicine, and business. Consumer demand for realistic animation, including virtual reality, is driving job growth in this highly competitive field.

DID YOU KNOW?

Forensic animators re-create crime and accident scenes. Used in court, such animation helped convict Michael Serge, a retired police officer, of murdering his wife in 2001. The animation used crime scene data to build an animated video showing how Serge could have shot his wife and then planted the knife he had said she used to attack him.

ON THE JOB

Much of your work as an animator will include working with established characters and **storyboards** or with original ones you develop. As a member of a team with artists and other animators, you use **scanners** and animation software to help bring a series of still drawings to life. For some projects, you pose models, puppets, or other objects and use **stop-motion** animation to make them appear to move. In others, you use computer-generated software. Feedback from directors, other animators, and clients helps you improve your work. You consider a variety of ways to input their ideas and then ask for additional feedback. No matter how many changes people request, you still try to deliver the project on time, even if that means working long hours.

Medical animation can teach professionals and their patients about specific conditions.

WHAT CAN YOU DO NOW?

Develop your art skills by joining an art club or taking sketching or cartooning classes. Learn all you can about the different kinds of animation and the materials and tools that animators use. Experiment with simple animations by learning how to use programs such as Pencil2D or CreaToon. Search online for tutorials and activites to practice your skills. Surprise family members or friends with a computer animation of them signed by the artist—you!

DID YOU KNOW?

In 2015, more than half of all animators were self-employed.

YOUR PATH TO WORK AS AN ANIMATOR

SECONDARY SCHOOL

Focus on math, art, computer, science, and social studies courses.

POST-SECONDARY

A college or university degree in animation is advised.

How does your favorite game's animation contribute to your pleasure in playing it?

Engineers use computer animation to help them eliminate design problems before they build a **prototype**.

WEB
DEVELOPER

Web developers take the visions of web designers and make them real.

Much planning goes into the development of a website. The easier the site is for users to **navigate**, the more successful it will be.

This web developer works in WordPress, a software that powers 24 percent of the world's websites.

Websites are used in many ways. There are information sites, **e-commerce** sites, social network sites, and entertainment sites that offer movie streaming and music downloads. With more and more sites appearing every day, it is no surprise that the field of web design continues to grow.

ON THE JOB

As a web developer, you work closely with web designers. You create website **layouts** for web designers' ideas, including an outline of how people will interact with the site. You develop the site using software, and maintain backup files in case something goes wrong. You update all information regularly. During development, you use **search engine optimization** to maximize the number of people sent to the site by search engines. You monitor how well the site works for various users and improve, expand, and upgrade the software when needed. With the help of security experts, you also install online security.

THE WORKPLACE

With the popularity of e-commerce, web developers have a choice of places to work. Some develop sales sites for manufacturers, schools and colleges, or other businesses. Others work on service sites for government agencies and financial institutions.

WHAT CAN YOU DO NOW?

Experiment with planning and developing your own personal website using a free service such as Tumblr. Experiment with ways to drive traffic to the site by repeating certain words or phrases.

YOUR PATH TO WORK AS A WEB DEVELOPER

SECONDARY SCHOOL

Math, computer science, science, and art courses are a great start.

POST-SECONDARY

A college or university degree in computer programming or computer software development is required.

DID YOU KNOW?

In 2015, there were about 650,000 e-commerce sites that sold at least $1,000 of merchandise. Web design was the difference between profitable and unprofitable sites for this market that is expected to be worth $27 trillion by 2020.

DID YOU KNOW?

Amanda Lui is a web designer based in Los Angeles, California. She currently works at Walt Disney Imagineering—the birthplace of all Disney theme parks!

The Webby Awards are handed out every year to award website excellence. At the 2017 Webby Awards, the Best User Experience website winner was In Space We Trust.

1979
SEPTEMBER

PIONEER 11
THE FIRST SPACECRAFT
FLEW BY SATURN

DIONE   RHEA

TEPHIS   TITAN

ENCELADUS

MIMAS   EARTH

1981
APR
12

SHUTTLE COLUMBIA
THE FIRST REUSABLE
SPACECRAFT

SATURN

GAME
DESIGNER

Video game designers collaborate with teams of artists and programmers as they work together to bring the designer's vision to reality.

What's your favorite video game? Do you want to create and explore your own world in Minecraft? Or would you rather manage a zoo in Zoo Tycoon or run a farm in Farm Simulator? The popularity of action, adventure, role-playing, and strategy games, as well as continued sales for classic titles such as Super Mario, means that openings for video game designers continue to grow.

By the middle of 2016, 495 million copies of Tetris had been sold, making it the top-selling video game of all time.

ON THE JOB

As a video game designer, you work with a team of people to develop the kind of game you'd like to play. You think up new ideas. You write detailed descriptions that include the plot, characters, and game play. Then you create rough storyboards and meet with team members to discuss what you've done and get feedback. Once you've developed something that you and the others are happy with, you work with artists and programmers to bring the design to life. As you have fun playing the game prototype, you assess the game for its entertainment value. Is it irresistible? If it isn't, you rethink the design and keep working on ideas until you have one that's hard to turn off. That's the winner. Then you write manuals and hint books for users.

Storyboards show the main action of games.

DID YOU KNOW?

Emotion recognition software allows a game to analyze a player's facial expressions! What happens in the game will change based on what emotions the software picks up.

WHAT CAN YOU DO NOW?

Research and study the history of video game design. Play a lot of different video games. Decide which games are your favorite and what it is about the designs of these games that most appeals to you. Try making your own game using free software such as Construct 2. Join a gaming club or start one of your own.

DID YOU KNOW?

As chief marketing officer for Rovio Entertainment, Blanca Juti is the driver behind the popularity of Angry Birds.

YOUR PATH TO WORK AS A GAME DESIGNER

SECONDARY SCHOOL

Focus on math, computer science, science, and art.

POST-SECONDARY

A college certificate or degree in game design, game development, computer science, or art is advised.

These video game designers discuss an early prototype of their most recent creation. How can they make the game so good that players won't want to stop?

SOFTWARE
DEVELOPER

Software developers create the programs and applications that make using computers so easy and so much fun.

If you have suggestions for improving Siri or some new ideas for the use of voice recognition software, then you might make a great software developer. The number of jobs in this field is expected to rise up to 17 percent over the next few years with the continued high demand for computer software that can do everything from stream music to Instagram thoughts and ideas.

ON THE JOB

As a software developer, you work with a team to generate software that allows people to do specific tasks on a computer, mobile phone, or other device. In most companies, you start by analyzing user needs. Then you design, test, and develop software to meet these needs. This includes assessing what security might be needed and planning that as part of the package. You create models or diagrams to show programmers how to write **computer code** for your idea. Once you have a prototype, you test it, listen to user feedback, and improve or simplify the program to make it more usable. You keep notes on each step in the process so that you know exactly what's been done if you need to make future fixes or upgrades.

Talkitt translates unintelligible speech so that others can understand it. This allows people with motor and speech disorders to communicate.

THE WORKPLACE

Although many software developers work for computer systems design companies, computer manufactures, and software publishers, some may work at a bank, insurance company, or electronic product manufacturer.

WHAT CAN YOU DO NOW?

Learn all you can about software design. Join a computing club. Volunteer to assist people with their computer equipment.

This software developer starts to block out ideas for a mobile app.

YOUR PATH TO WORK AS A SOFTWARE DEVELOPER

SECONDARY SCHOOL

Focus on math, computer science, science, and social studies courses.

POST-SECONDARY

You will need a university degree in computer science, software engineering, mathematics, or a related field.

DID YOU KNOW?

Computer coding **bootcamps**, such as Galvanize, Grand Circus, Hackbright Academy, and Metis, are committed to encouraging diversity in the computer programming industry. They offer many scholarships to students, including African American, Latino, and female students. A 2015 report found that 89 percent of bootcamp grads had jobs within four months of graduation.

In 2017, the favorite app for 39 percent of American teens was Snapchat. Instagram was second at 23 percent.

COMPUTER SYSTEMS
ANALYST

Computer systems analysts design information systems to help businesses run more efficiently.

Coaches on the Atlanta Falcons football team use **GPS** technology to track player movements during practice and help them develop more effective plays. Netflix mines its extensive database of most-watched movies to help it make decisions about what new films to buy for its customers. These are just two examples of how computer systems analysts can increase the efficiency and profitability of any business.

ON THE JOB

As a computer systems analyst, you investigate a company's current computer systems and procedures. You listen to managers and assess how IT might help the organization. Then you choose or design applications that help the organization run more efficiently. For example, you might suggest moving certain information onto the **cloud** to make it available to employees 24/7, no matter where they are. Once decisions are made, you choose and **configure** new hardware and software. For best results, you **customize** them for your organization. You then test the new systems to make sure they work as expected and troubleshoot problems. You train employees in the use of the new systems, and you may write instruction manuals.

THE WORKPLACE

Some analysts work for large consulting firms that hire them out to government agencies or corporations to complete specific projects.

WHAT CAN YOU DO NOW?

Research and study how computer systems operate. Search online for tutorials or activities to increase your knowledge. Join a computing club. Volunteer to keep the computers of friends and relatives running smoothly.

The Houston Astros baseball team uses IT to assess players and make in-game decisions. The programs work so well that the team won the 2017 World Series.

Computer systems analysts help businesses run more efficiently.

YOUR PATH TO WORK AS A COMPUTER SYSTEMS ANALYST

SECONDARY SCHOOL

Math, computer, science, social studies, and business courses are advised.

POST-SECONDARY

You will need a college or university degree in computing, information science, or business.

DID YOU KNOW?

Using the Mark43 web app, police officers can fill in incident and arrest reports in half the time it normally takes. The app connects crime reports to social media and phone records, giving police a better picture of criminal activity.

Analysts have developed computerized tools, including drones, to help farmers better plan the planting, fertilizing, and watering of their crops.

LEARNING MORE

BOOKS

Gregory, Josh. *Animation: From Concept to Consumer*. Scholastic Library Publishing, 2015.

Gregory, Josh. *Apps: From Concept to Consumer*. Scholastic Library Publishing, 2015.

Mason, Helen. *What is Digital Entrepreneurship?* Crabtree Publishing Company, 2017.

WEBSITES

WWW.CAREEROUTLOOK.US/ ASSESSMENT/SHORT.SHTML	Career Outlook	Check how your personal interests relate to the world of work. Find out the minimum education and growth outlook for each job.
WWW.LIFEVALUESINVENTORY. ORG/THE-PROCESS.HTML	Life Values Inventory	Consider your personal values. What occupations might these lead to?
WWW.KENT.AC.UK/CAREERS/ SK/CARDS5.HTML	Employability Skills Game	Match skill descriptions with the word that describes the skill.
WWW.IDTECH.COM/COURSES	Tech Camp	Find a tech course that suits your location and budget.

GLOSSARY

adaptor A device for connecting pieces of equipment that cannot be connected directly

application A computer program that performs tasks

apprenticeship A period of time spent learning skilled work with hands-on training

bootcamp A short and intense course of training

certification Certificate that shows someone has achieved a certain level of skill and knowledge

Cloud Refers to storage services on the Internet

configure Arrange or order a computer system so that it is suitable for a specific task

computer code A series of symbols in a computer program that provide instructions for it to run

critical error A computer error that prevents a program from working

customize To modify something to suit a particular task

cyber attack A malicious act against computer systems, networks, or devices in an effort to steal, alter, or destroy devices or information

database A set of data stored in a computer system

e-commerce Commercial transactions conducted online

encryption Process of converting data or information into a code, usually to prevent unauthorized use

firewall Part of a computer system to prevent unauthorized use

forensic To apply scientific knowledge to legal problems

GPS Short form for Global Positioning System. A navigation system allowing users to determine their exact location at all times.

hacker A person who illegally gains access to computer systems

hardware The interior parts of a computer

Indigenous The original occupants of a land

interactive A two-way flow of information between a computer and the user

keylogger virus A virus that picks up every keystroke on an infected machine

layout Sketch of how parts of a system will be arranged and connected

multimedia Content that includes a variety of forms, such as audio, text, and animation

navigate To operate a system or make one's way through

network A system of computers connected by communication lines

postproduction The work done on a movie after filming has taken place

prototype First model of something that is made and tested to see how the final item might be improved

ransomware Harmful software used to block access to a computer system until money has been paid

remote access Ability to get access to a computer or computer network from a distance

router A small electronic device that joins networks together using either cables or wireless connections

scanner A device that copies documents and turns them into computer files

search engine optimization Making sure a website address appears early in search engine results

security breach When private or protected information is copied, viewed, stolen, communicated, or used by unauthorized people

software Programs that are added to a computer system

stock exchange An organized system for financial trading

stop-motion A technique in which objects are photographed in slightly altered positions. The images are then shown in rapid succession, to give the appearance of movement.

storyboard Drawings representing the scenes planned for a production

teleconferencing Multiple people in different locations being able to communicate together through telephone or computer systems

INDEX